old wive~
sheep's-hea~   ~,
sausages an~ sago

carol cooke

© Carol Cooke

ISBN 1 901888 38 X

First published 2004

Cover Design Mark Whitley

Illustrations including Cover Illustration by Sheila Graber

Published in Great Britain by
Business Education Publishers Limited
The Teleport
Doxford International
Sunderland
SR3 3XD

Tel: 0191 5252410
Fax: 0191 5201815

British Cataloguing-in-Publications Data
A catalogue record for this book is available from the British Library.

Printed in Great Britain by the Alden Group, Oxford.

Content

To my mother, Lilian Bianchi, who told me stories about cooking and laughed at the ridiculous nature of it all

Foreword

'The past is a foreign country, they do things different there.' Nowhere is that truer than when you talk about food. My mother was raised in the Lake District and one of her favourite delicacies was tatie hash. Now tatie hash was a sort of lamb stewy type thing. I use the word 'lamb' loosely because I'm not sure that any sheep younger than thirty five was ever allowed to be used in its manufacture. There were potatoes, boiled to destruction, a lot of water and some floating hunks of neck end of mutton, still on the bone needless to say and somehow or other with more attached fragments of fat than the animal can ever have had when alive. My mother and sister loved it but I hated it and the only thing to be said in its favour is that it wasn't sheep's-head broth! How I was taken back to those days when I read Carol's salutary reminder of the astonishing ways we used to eat. I bet this book will bring back similar memories for you.

John Grundy

Introduction

Our grandparents and parents were accustomed to doing a full day's work before breakfast. Men traditionally worked in heavy industry, shipbuilding, coal mining, construction work and farming, while women had to contend with kids, cooking, housework and shopping, without the washing machines, dryers, dishwashers and other paraphernalia which we consider, rightly in my view, to be essential.

In addition to looking after children, and running up and down the back stairs with loads of wet laundry, women also had to concoct nourishing and hot food, often on a black range fireplace with unsophisticated heating controls. Women provided much of the day to day food, and also found the energy to rustle up delicacies for special occasions.

My mother was always a good cook, so I was never interested in entering the kitchen until I was fifteen years old and attending the Girls Grammar School in South Shields. My German exam results were disastrous, and my German teacher was less than enthusiastic about my continuing to decline German verbs. I was led to Miss Willie, the Domestic Science teacher, and her dog Chalky. Miss Willie reigned over the cookery block and the flat. The flat sounded very glamorous but was really only a couple of rooms which you had to learn how to keep clean. The flat cleaning bit was not desperately appealing and the cooking hardly more so. Everyone made brown stew, and those who were more sophisticated progressed to beef casserole – same thing, different name. Before brown stew though, we were taught to toast bread and also how to boil an egg. Elementary you might think, but Delia Smith took this very skill as her starting point in her book entitled, *How to boil an egg*. So perhaps Miss Willie wasn't too far wide of the mark.

I eventually gained the giddy heights of O' level Domestic Science. My mother was also taking a Northern Counties Home Economics cookery course at the Marine and Technical College South Shields, so talk in our house consisted of discussions on roux sauces and the 'rubbing in method'. I had to cook a vegetarian menu for my exam, and eventually delivered up an egg and cheese flan, followed by a chocolate mousse, which relied heavily on evaporated milk and very little else.

This meal was judged by all to be well balanced and tasty – at first! But in order to get this menu cooked to perfection, I had several trial runs at home, where my family were forced to eat egg and cheese flan and chocolate mousse, three Sundays in a row.

Later my sister also took the Domestic Science route. She didn't suffer the indignity of being thrown out of the German class; she was thrown out of the Latin class. When the time came for her exam, guess what she had to cook? A vegetarian menu. It seemed to work for me – so why shouldn't it work for her? She chose egg and cheese flan and chocolate mousse. The family ate egg and cheese flan and chocolate mousse for three more Sundays running.

When my other sister was approaching exam time, my parents asked her to stick in and try to get into the Latin group. It wasn't that they thought that Latin was a particularly good subject to be studying…they were just sick and tired of that vegetarian menu, and knew, without a shadow of a doubt, that they could not suffer the flan and mousse combo one more time.

Whatever the merits of vegetarian flan and mousse, the cookery course did teach me the basics, and this, clearly, is very important. *Enquire within upon Everything*, a weighty and self confident manual, full of good advice to householders, published at the turn of the century by Houlston and Sons of Paternoster Square, London states the following:

> *Nothing is more important in the affairs of housekeeping than the choice of wholesome food.*

Writing and researching this book gave me the chance to read old cookery books, which are brimming with good advice and offer us a valuable insight into how people lived and thought. The 'Empire Christmas Pudding' is assured in the knowledge that there will always be a British Empire, and that the food from the Empire belongs to us, the British, to use as we see fit. Other recipes show how industrious and hard working people were. Shining through many of these recipes is the fact that although people didn't have much money, they were prepared to work hard and do the best for their families.

I've also had the opportunity to talk to people about a topic which interests them, their past, their families, and their households. Most people have warm memories of childhood, and these memories often centre on food. Preparing food for people you love is a way of showing that you care, and are prepared take trouble and time to give them the best.

A bit of sound advice

Nourishing food, lots of it and served on the table at regular intervals were important in keeping the family running smoothly and without incident. Indeed a weighty tome called *News Chronicle – Everything Within. A Library of Information for the Home* has this to say about the importance of cooking:

> *In any household, large or small, both the health and wellbeing of the members of the family depend upon cooking and catering, and the kitchen is one of the most vital departments of the home, the wife's own workshop and the mainspring of domestic affairs.*

Everything Within has no time for doubts or equivocation, the section continues with the words:

> *A constant variation of diet, quite apart from the ever-changing seasons, is of the utmost importance, and everything depends upon the wise choice of food, its preparation, its freshness and sound quality – conditions of spotless cleanliness being essential.*

Yes, but is it seasonal?

It is interesting to note that the seasons played a large part in determining what people ate. In *Modern Cookery Illustrated* published in the 1950s, we find a year's supply of menus, one for each day of the week. Summer menus are heavy on salad, strawberries, jellied fruit and delicacies like Morello Cherry sponge, while a typical week of winter recipes focus heavily on delicious dishes which we only dream about today, like Mincemeat Roly-Poly, Baked Orange Pudding, or Jam Layer Pudding.

Today we don't worry too much about when we can get food. We eat salad all year round and on the rare occasions when we can't find fresh fruit, then we can get it frozen. This is great; the only problem is that tomatoes taste of nothing, and frozen strawberries and 'rasps', as my granny called raspberries, taste of iced water.

Sample menu – Winter

Let me give you a sample day of recipes from *Modern Cookery Illustrated* and see how you'd like to do this amount of cooking everyday, then estimate the size you would be if you did this much eating everyday, particularly as we tend not to build piers, like my great-grandfather, hew coal, like my grandfather, or work in the white hot heat of an iron foundry like my father-in-law. Desk jobs can be tough but they don't burn off those calories in quite the same efficient way.

Winter recipes – Fourth week

Breakfast – Cereal, sausages and fried apples.

Dinner – Roast leg of mutton, red currant or cranberry jelly, roast potatoes, mashed parsnips, apricot tart and custard.

Supper – Celery soup, stuffed potatoes, lemon blancmange, stewed pears.

Accustomed as I am to serving 'chicken ting' – bung it in the microwave and wait for it to 'ting' – I am amazed at one day's menus, and that's just a pretty ho-hum day, nothing special you understand. I count eleven processes which the cook would have to take on, during a busy day, in order to get this menu on the table. This isn't counting pouring the cereal into a bowl and adding milk, nor the preparing of vegetables, and the shopping. Just the processes. You would no sooner get one lot of food cleared away than have to start on the next.

Sample menu – Summer

A typical summer menu was hardly less strenuous, both on the part of the cook, and the person who was required to eat such a vast and complex amount of food.

Modern Cookery Illustrated suggests the following tips for success:

> *Introduce as much variety in your menus as possible. It is*
> *a good plan to try some new dish every week…which*
> *will soon prove a firm favourite with the family.*

Summer – First week – Monday

Breakfast – Fresh fruit, cold gammon, brown bread and honey.

Dinner – Braised veal, carrots and onions, new potatoes, lemon pudding.

Supper – Eggs in mayonnaise sauce, tomato salad, jellied fruit tarts.

On the face of it, this day's recipes sound a bit easier to achieve, then you look at it and wonder. Who would have a bit of gammon ready first thing on a Monday morning – especially if you had just got the washing started? Who would have time to prepare three vegetables and a cooked lemon pudding, as well as watching out for the showers of rain and the coalman, once the washing had been hung out? Who would have time to make, from scratch, mayonnaise for the eggs and pastry for the fruit tarts – no fridge or freezer containing frozen pastry made earlier.

Truly, women were made of stern stuff. Never mind the cooking and the washing, it's a wonder they didn't faint at the thought of mayonnaise.

Meat

Steak and kidney pudding

Steak and kidney seems to be regarded with affection by all. It was regarded as a good meal for a winter day, and not too troublesome to cook. My granny had a system for buying her meat. She called at the butcher's shop, ordered a couple of days worth of meat, such as steak and kidney and a piece of beef, to be delivered by the butcher boy on a bicycle, and then asked her butcher, a Welshman called Mr Bartlett, if he would put something in the parcel that he thought they'd like.

He always did and they always did.

The recipe

> 1 lb lean backskirt steak and kidney
> 12 oz plain flour
> 6 oz grated suet
> Pinch of salt
>
> Mix the flour and suet with cold water to make a very firm pastry.

Grease a three pint basin.

Roll out two thirds of pastry to line the pudding dish, leaving one third, to be rolled out into a circle to form the top of the pudding.

Cut the steak into small pieces and roll in flour.

Remove the core from the kidney and cut into pieces.

Roll in flour and add both meat and kidney to lined basin.

Mix Simmington's gravy salt with water and pour over the meat in the basin.

Flour from the steak will make thick gravy.

Cover with suet lid and seal.

Cover with greased grease-proof paper and a sealed pudding cloth – muslin, coated with flour and sprinkled with water to make a paste, tie well with string.

This dish requires steaming in a steamer over continually boiling water for up to four hours, remembering to add more boiling water to the saucepan.

Root vegetables could be cooked in the pan underneath the steamer.

The dish sounds great and could be made today, but who would devote four hours to steaming one dish?

Guinness and steak and kidney pudding

Yon Lawson remembers her grandmother, Ellen Robertshaw, making a similar pudding but instead of cooking it in an enamel pudding dish, she used to tie the pudding up in a muslin cloth and immerse the whole thing in water. Yon said, 'I make the pie occasionally, using a cloth that belonged to my grandmother.' Ellen sounds a bit of a character. She lived in the Mariner's Cottages in North Shields, near the Rising Sun pub on the Coast Road and liked to visit the pub with an earthenware jug, buy half a pint of Guinness then take it home to drink. Her husband wasn't very happy about this notion so in order to curb her activities, he would hide her shoes. Ellen got the better of him though; she kept a pair of velvet slippers, also well hidden, so that even if her shoes disappeared, she still had the slippers to wear for her journey to the pub.

Sheep's-head broth

Sheep's-head broth is scary. Have you ever seen a sheep's-head, not running around a field, but on a butcher's slab, devoid of any of that curly white hair and melting brown eyes? The first time I saw a sheep's-head I had nightmares and it hasn't got any better. The most appalling thing for me is the fact that the sheep's-head is red, bony and still has teeth. Horror movie makers should look no further. Sheep's-head broth making is much more frightening than *The Night of the Living Dead*. However, the recipe allows me to tell a couple of stories and my favourite joke.

Sheep's-head broth

The recipe

Lilian Bianchi of South Shields remembers her mother cooking this dish, and says:

> A very substantial meal was broth made with a lamb's head. The butcher would split and trim the head. The head was then brought home and washed thoroughly, particularly the nose. The teeth then had to be rubbed with salt and the brain washed, any fibre removed, tied in muslin and boiled gently in slightly salted water for an hour. The head was soaked in salt water overnight and then put in a large enamel bowl which would fit into the coal oven.

> Four ounces of barley, four ounces of split peas and four ounces of dried peas were added after soaking overnight, then the whole lot was covered completely with five pints of water and seasoned with salt and pepper.

> After two hours cubed carrots, turnip, potatoes, or any other seasonal root vegetable, like parsnip and leek amounting to two pound in weight, were added.

> After about three hours the head would be removed and the quantity of fluid was adjusted. The soup at that point was often very firm because the barley would absorb much of the fluid.

> At this point dumplings, made with eight ounces of self raising flour and four ounces of grated suet and a pinch of salt, mixed to a fairly firm dough and rolled into little balls, were added, along with the brain in the bag. This was cooked for a further thirty minutes.

Parsley (if available) could be added to the cooked broth for colour and nutrients.

According to my mother, 'The brain was considered by many to be a delicacy, but in our house only my father Louis Clark enjoyed it, on toast, for supper.' I for one wouldn't be fighting him for that privilege.

However, the dish was obviously very efficient for not only were the head and brains used, but the tongue was also pressed into service. The sheep's-tongue was removed and put in a small bowl with a plate on top and a flat iron on top of that. The resulting pressed tongue was skinned and sliced for a nice sandwich later in the day, together with the rest of the meat taken from the sheep's-head. The whole Clark family enjoyed the tongue.

And remember, if you kept the sheep's-eyes, they would see you through the rest of the week!

The stories

Joyce Telford of South Shields remembers visiting the home of her boyfriend John, when they were courting, in the 1950s. His mother had made a very nice tea and encouraged Joyce to take several sandwiches. After eating a sandwich Joyce, wanting to be polite and impress her future in-laws, said 'That was nice. What was it?' Mrs Telford answered 'Sheep's-brains.' Joyce can still remember feeling very sick, even though the sandwiches had been tasty.

Ruth Hearn remembers her father baking a sheep's-head in the oven, in the 1950s, and can still hear the shrieks of panic when someone opened the oven and encountered the baking head, complete with teeth and eyes.

More recently, I was discussing the gruesomeness of old recipes, and a woman informed me that she had been on holiday to a hotel in Norway, where half a smoked sheep's-head is considered to be something of a delicacy. Guests are encouraged to dress up in evening dress and black tie, in honour of the sheep's-head, then the dish is served accompanied by Schnapps.

The joke

A man walks into a butchers shop and says to the woman behind the counter, 'Have you got a sheep's-head pet?' and the woman replies, 'No, it's just the way I part my hair.' Well, it always makes me laugh.

Calf's foot soup

It wasn't only sheep who had to look out for their heads, calves also had to keep a weather-eye out for people trying to make soup out of their feet. Here is a recipe for such soup, from *Modern Cookery Illustrated*.

The recipe

    1 calf's foot
    3 pints water
    1 piece lemon rind
    1 small ham or bacon bone or slice of lean ham

1 sprig each of thyme, marjoram and savory
6 peppercorns
Scrap of mace
1 small carrot
1 onion
1 pint of milk
Yolk of 1 egg
Parsley

Time 3 hours on first day; 30 minutes on second day.

Wash calf's foot and cut into pieces, put in stewpan with strip of lemon rind, ham – or failing that a good teaspoon of salt, the herbs and vegetables cut into small pieces.

Bring to the boil and skim well. Simmer slowly for three hours. Strain in a bowl and leave until the next day.

Remove all fat, put the jelly in the stewpan with a few pieces of meat cut into small pieces, bring to the boil then take off the stove. Beat the yolk of an egg with a tablespoon of milk, stir in a little of the hot broth then pour into the stewpan and heat. Sprinkle with chopped parsley and serve.

The book goes on to point out the positive benefits of this soup:

> *This soup has a high nutrition value, and is easily digested. It is particularly good for invalids and delicate people, and, when cold will form a thick jelly which is also delicious. The long slow cooking brings out its goodness to the full. It also has the advantage of being very cheap to prepare.*

What strikes me about this recipe is how sophisticated it is. The cook would have to use several herbs, and also blend in milk and eggs without them curdling. Not easy, not quick, but I presume delicious as the recipe says.

A few broth

Broth could be made with anything and often was. Stock from the meat and whatever vegetables were to hand made a very nice broth which could be made even tastier with the addition of some suet dumplings, made later and dropped into the broth, simmered gently for twenty minutes then eaten piping hot. Delicious. Aside from being great, the nice thing about broth is that my nana used to say, 'I'll make a few broth.' You don't hear that much nowadays.

Musician Ron Simpson, remembered his mother making Scotch broth which was cooked for days on end. It was possible, with the fire-back ovens, to have stock simmering constantly, then for a few vegetables and meat to be tossed into the stock-pot, and a very cheap and nourishing meal to be served a few hours later. Top restaurants today have obviously learned a thing or two from the stock-pot system of cooking, for many restaurants have a stock-pot on the go the whole time. Just check with Raymond Blanc if you don't believe me.

Pig's ears

It seems as if no part of any animal was safe from the experienced cook. In a book called *Warne's Model Cookery and Housekeeping Book* published in May 1868 and sold for one shilling, we find that pig's ears were a delicacy much coveted for breakfast. The recipe is as follows:

The recipe

 2 pig's ears
 1 anchovy
 1 teaspoon of sage and parsley
 ¼ lb of suet, finely chopped
 5 oz of breadcrumbs
 Salt and pepper
 2 eggs
 2 oz of butter
 ½ pint of rich gravy
 1 glass sherry
 3 teaspoons of made mustard
 A piece of butter
 1 teaspoon of flour
 1 small onion
 Pinch of cayenne pepper

Parboil the ears, make a forcemeat stuffing of anchovy, sage, parsley, suet, breadcrumbs, pepper and salt. Mix and bind with beaten yolks of two eggs. Raise the skin of the upper side of the ears, and stuff them with it. Fry the ears in fresh butter to a nice brown. Pour away the fat and drain them.

Make the following gravy: add to half a pint of rich stock or gravy, a glass of sherry, three tablespoons of made mustard, butter rolled in flour, small onion whole, and half a salt spoonful of white pepper. Put this gravy, with the ears, into a stewpan, and cover; stew gently for half an hour, shaking it often. Then take out the onion, place the ears carefully in a dish, and pour the sauce over them. If you require more than two ears, the same quantity of sauce will do for four.

This recipe is followed by a recipe for cooking 'pig's feet and ears', 'pig's feet soused' and 'pig's kidneys', and several people I talked to remember eating pig's trotters accompanied by mustard and vinegar, with enormous enjoyment.

When times are hard and money scarce, it is clearly important not to waste any part of an animal which might provide a warm and nutritious meal. None of the recipes do much for me, but I admire the fortitude of the bygone cook who thought it would be a great idea to take a pair of pig's ears and stuff them – what creativity, what nerve, what a weird idea!

Mock kidney soup

While browsing through *Everything Within* I came upon this astonishing recipe for 'Mock kidney soup'. I found it astonishing because I couldn't imagine why anyone might want to make soup out of kidneys. However if they were set on the project, surely it would be sensible to find out if it were possible to buy kidneys, and if not then make something else. Presumably at one time people were so keen on kidney soup, that they were willing to make it out of something else rather than not eat it at all.

The recipe

> 1 quart good vegetable stock – season rather highly,
> strain and skim well.
>
> Boil ½ lb liver for thirty minutes, cool and dice.
>
> Melt one tablespoon dripping and brown liver well, add
> the stock and simmer for two hours, thickening with one
> tablespoon cornflour mixed to a paste with water.
>
> A tablespoon of Yorkshire Relish should be added just
> before serving.

So there you have it – mock kidney soup is made with liver. Why it should be easier to get liver rather than kidney I don't know. When an animal is killed there is presumably one liver and two kidneys, so you could be forgiven for thinking that it would be easier to buy kidneys rather than liver. The answer to the problem is lost in the mists of time. It is possible that the soulution arose because it was difficult to get certain foodstuffs, like eggs and fruit, as it was a time of deprivation, but why that should apply to kidneys and not livers is beyond me.

Rolled lap

Another dish which you don't hear a lot about today is lap. Lap is one of the cheaper cuts of lamb and although the meat is rather greasy it is apparently very tasty.

The recipe

Get a lean piece of lap from the butcher.

Lay the meat out flat and place ½ lb of sausage meat and some sage and a large chopped onion on to the meat.

Roll up the meat and tie with string, then put in a baking dish and cook in a moderate oven for 1½ hours.

Ron Simpson remembered that his mother used to fry or oven bake lap so that it became crispy and very enjoyable indeed.

Bible tripe

Mrs Ann Edgar of Chester-le-Street, aged ninety seven, remembers her mother cooking cowheel and tripe as a dinner dish. She says that it was very gelatinous and after you had eaten it, your lips would be stuck together. She loved tripe and cooked it in milk, with onions, then served it with bread and butter, as a supper dish.

Mrs Edgar remembers that there were different kinds of tripe. One type was called 'Bible Tripe' because it looked like a huge bible, having a thick ridge which was very tough, like a book spine, with flaps that looked like the pages of a bible.

For those sensitive souls like me, who have been protected from eating tripe, and are always a bit unsure about where it came from and what is was doing, tripe is a cow's stomach, and was once both a very popular and nourishing food. Plain tripe was taken from the cow's rumen (first stomach) and honeycomb tripe from the reticulum (second stomach). It was often eaten cold with salt pepper and vinegar or cooked with onions.

Reed tripe

Ron Simpson remembered that people used to buy pig's trotters in tripe shops, ready cooked to be eaten immediately, a bit like our fast food now. However the tripe shop also sold foods like slut, a type of tripe found mainly in Manchester for some reason, sweetbreads and reed tripe. Margaret Quinn of South Shields says that her mother-in-law taught her how to cook reed tripe. It sounds a bit off-putting to me as Margaret says, 'It was grey and wrinkly but tasted wonderful when poached gently, in a pan, or in a low oven, with milk.'

The recipe

Plain white tripe could be sliced then dipped in a thin batter made from:

1 oz butter
1 oz flour
½ pint milk
Good pinch of salt

Melt the butter in a pan over a very gentle heat then gradually stir in the flour, making sure that the mixture remains smooth. Add the salt and continue stirring until all of the flour has been absorbed by the butter. Then add the milk gradually, stirring well, over a gentle heat, until all the milk has been absorbed into the flour paste. This sauce is called a 'white roux' and can be used as the basis for many sauces, both sweet and savoury. The tripe was then dropped into the roux sauce and coated with the batter, then shallow fried. The result was said to be wonderful for your stomach.

Although I can't pretend to like tripe, or even want to see other people eating it, tripe isn't just a northern delicacy but has been prepared and eaten around the world for centuries. Artusi (1820-1911) a passionate Italian cook, who entertained many of the leading figures of his time and whose cook book has been printed in Italy since 1891, says:

> *No matter how it's cooked, tripe is an ordinary dish. I find it poorly suited to delicate digestions, though this is perhaps less true if it is cooked in the Milanese style, which renders it tender and light...*

(Source: http://italianfood.about.com)

Sweetbreads

Sweetbreads were a delicacy which could be bought cheaply at the butchers. The sweetbreads would be scalded to remove the sinewy sacks, and then covered in water and poached in a pan with onions and carrots for flavour. Just before serving a dash of milk, or even cream would be added.

Enquire within upon Everything has this to say about sweetbreads:

> *Trim a fine sweetbread (it cannot be too fresh) parboil it*
> *for five minutes and throw it into a basin of cold water.*
> *Then roast it plain – or beat up the yolk of an egg, and*
> *prepare some fine breadcrumbs; or when the sweetbread is*
> *cold, dry it thoroughly in a cloth; run a larkspit or a*
> *skewer through it and tie it on an ordinary spit; egg it*
> *with a pastebrush and roast it.*

The reader is then given more ideas about sauces to serve with the skewered sweetbread, 'For sauce, melted butter, lemon juice or serve on buttered toast with gravy.'

For those who don't know, a larkspit was an implement for cooking small birds. The hook, at one end, would go over the front of a roaring fire and the birds would hang two at a time, from small hooks which could be moved backwards and forwards along the handle to get them the right distance from the flames.

Black pudding

Warne's Model Cookery and Housekeeping Book adopts a very jaunty attitude to cooking. No matter how difficult or distasteful the dish might appear, this little volume tackles it with enthusiasm and a can-do attitude which puts us to shame today. Here is their recipe for black pudding:

The recipe

Time to soak – one night.
To boil – half an hour.
Rather more than 1 quart of blood[1]
1 quart of whole groats[2]
Crumb of a quartern loaf
2 quarts of new milk
Small bunch of winter savory and thyme
2 teaspoons salt
1 teaspoon pepper
6 cloves
½ teaspoon of allspice, nutmeg, little grated ginger
3 lb beef suet
6 eggs
3 oz of pork fat

Stir the hot blood with salt till it is quite cold, put a quart of it or rather more to a quart of whole groats, to soak one night. Soak the crumb of the quartern loaf in rather more than two quarts of new milk made hot. Chop fine a little winter savory and thyme, beat up and strain six eggs; chop three pounds of beef suet, the herbs, and the seasoning of pepper, salt, allspice, cloves, ginger and nutmeg together with the eggs. Then add it to and beat with it the groats and soaked bread. When well mixed, have ready some skin bags, as for sausages, but much

---

[1] A quart is an imperial liquid or dry measure equal to two pints or 1.136 litres.

[2] Oats were inexpensive to buy and could be a real boon to people trying to achieve a good diet on a low budget. Available as groats (whole grains with the husks removed).

larger (we suppose, of course, that they have been well cleaned and soaked). Put the mixture into these bags, but as you do so add at regular distances, pork fat cut into large dice. Tie the skins in links only half-filled, and boil the puddings in a large kettle, pricking them as they swell, or they will burst. When boiled, dry them in clean cloths and hang them up.

To cook them for eating, scald them for a few minutes in water and cook them in a Dutch oven[3].

Bacon and sausage hot pot

This dish was a winner because it could be prepared, put in the oven, and then left while the cook went shopping. Maureen Ainley of South Shields says 'My mother used to make bacon and sausage hot pot for lunch on a Saturday.'

The recipe

Line the casserole dish with a layer of sliced potatoes, and then add a layer of onions and carrots, with enough water, seasoned with salt and pepper, to cover the vegetables. Cover the layers with sausages, still in their skins, then add another layer of sliced potatoes and finish off by covering the whole lot with strips of bacon. Put in a moderate oven for 1½-2 hours. The lid could be taken off the casserole dish and the bacon browned off, ready to serve.

---

[3] Heavy cast iron three legged oven with a tight fitting lid.

Maureen adds that her mother, Evelyn Ogle would 'place the casserole in the oven, put on her smartest hat and catch the number thirty bus into the centre of South Shields where she would have a coffee and a chat with a friend in Binns café. She would then catch the bus back and be home just as the casserole finished cooking.'

Sadly Binns café is no longer in South Shields town centre, so there is no way of verifying that the timings were correct, but the shop lives on, in the memory of many Shields people.

The department store was the home of some very fancy designer clothes at one time, and I can remember as a little girl, being taken by my auntie Edna, to 'mannequin parades' in Binns café. We sat with some of my aunt's friends, watching the beautiful mannequins modelling gorgeous frocks, and longed for the end, when the best mannequin would emerge dressed as a bride, complete with bridegroom, followed by the rest of the mannequins done up as bridesmaids. How I longed to be that bride.

Sausage pie

Sausage pie was another handy dish which could be made, then ignored while the cook got on with something else. Jennifer Allen says that her mother Dorothy Morgan and her aunts, always made sausage pie on Christmas Eve. That way they could cook supper while making forcemeat stuffing for the turkey, and putting the final touches to preparations for Christmas Day.

The recipe

1½ lb sausage meat placed in a dish and browned off in
the oven. When partially cooked, pour off excess fat and
cover with sliced tomatoes and finish off with a layer of
mashed potatoes. Cover and return to a moderate oven
for about an hour. Just before serving, brown the top
layer, eat and wait for Santa.

Minced collops

I include this dish because I love the sound of the word 'collops'
although the meaning is fairly prosaic. Minced collops is traditionally
a Scottish dish using the best beef, minced, and is more commonly
known as 'mince and tatties'.

The recipe

2 lb of good rump steak, chopped fine
1 good sized onion, chopped fine

Put steak and onions into a pan with water or gravy to
cover the meat, then stir until the water begins to boil.
Simmer for ¾ hour, and just before serving, stir in a
tablespoon of flour, a little pepper and salt and boil.

Serve with mashed potatoes around the dish.

The Scots traditionally served their 'mince and tatties' with triangles
of hot toast.

Partridge pudding

One dish I am fairly certain you won't hear much about today is Partridge pudding, a dish I unearthed from a scrap-book of cut out recipes owned by Lyn Charlton's father, Louis Raymond Lowes. The scrap-book is an ancient exercise book crammed full of household hints, beauty tips and plain oddities; like how to clean patent leather slippers or use up old calendars. The exercise book is a family heirloom and was saved from destruction, in a fire, by Louis. The book was carefully collated and glued together by two sisters, Bessie and Kate Thompson, who used to own some land called Acklington Park in Northumberland.

The family farmed the land, in the 1800s, and also owned a woollen mill at the bottom of the bank, at Guizance. The woollen mill has now been turned into flats, but the recipe and household hints book, which contains one recipe for rhubarb wine dating back to 1862, has survived. Bessie was the last of the family and died in 1991, but her scrap-book lives on, a memento of times past, when it was important to know how to 'make stale bread new' or how to 'strengthen a garment'. The Thompson scrap-book contains this odd recipe for using up any old partridges you had hanging around the place.

The recipe

Rub an ounce of butter into seven ounces of flour, then add four ounces of grated suet, a half teaspoon of salt, a quarter teaspoon each of cream of tartar and bicarbonate of soda, and a level cup of cool or cold mashed potatoes. Use no liquid unless dry flour remains when well mixed.

Cut two or three (or more when plentiful) partridges into quarters, and make gravy from the backs and projecting bones. From old birds, strip off all skin. Add six or eight ounces of raw bacon in fine strips, season well and almost fill basin with good gravy. Steam or boil the pudding for three hours, placing grease-proof paper between lid of paste and cloth ties on top when boiling pudding. Mushrooms or sheep's-kidneys may replace bacon.

The recipe is probably served up in the best restaurants in London today, but I find it difficult to think about making a gravy from backs and projecting bones – way too graphic for me – or even stripping skin from old birds.

Lord Lampton's grouse

I've always had an uneasy relationship with the business of preparing, cooking and eating birds which I think stems from my close encounters with grouse. When I was young, my aunt worked for LNER (London North Eastern Railway), in the department which booked sleeping compartments for business people, on the London train. As a result of this activity, she had a series of fond and wealthy customers who were always keen to keep in her good books and be assured of a late reservation on the sleeper to London. Lord Lampton was just such a customer, and he used to show his appreciation of the sleeper booking activity by sending my aunt a brace of grouse killed at the start of the season. She would bring the grouse home, wrapped in brown paper, and sling them onto the table ready for my father to draw them, that is, take out the insides, and then pluck them. This was a signal for me and my sisters to flee the room. We hated dead birds, hated the drawing business, and didn't really like the idea of eating grouse – although we put that objection to one side as soon as they were cooked.

An additional hazard was the fact that before the birds could be cleaned, they had to be hung, so they were suspended on a hook in our scullery. I can still hear my screams as I wandered into the scullery to clean my shoes or head out to play in the back lane, only to be confronted with four bright beady eyes, turned upwards, hanging there, waiting for the oven.

Panhaggelty, panacklety, or panhaggerty!

And finally, on the subject of meat and how to cook it, no account of northern recipes would be complete without at least one recipe for panhaggelty, panacklety, or panhaggerty. Opinions differ widely as to how the dish is spelled and pronounced, but strangely, people seem to be united as to what panhaggelty, panacklety, or panhaggerty actually is.

I did some searching through old recipe books, and found a Scottish recipe for Pan Haggis pasted into The Thompson scrap-book. The recipe was clipped from a magazine column called 'What Aunt Ellen would Make'. The column is headed with a line drawing of an old lady, wearing wire rimmed spectacles, a checked apron, a black bombazine blouse with a cameo at the neck and a confident and caring smile. I think that Aunt Ellen is a bit too smartly dressed for a cooking session, but perhaps she doesn't throw flour about with as much abandon as me, and has better control over her rubbing-in method. Whatever the reason, Aunt Ellen looks great –

confident, calm, twinkly and relaxed. She is the precursor to all of those television cooks, from Fanny Craddock to Delia Smith, who inspire confidence just by their very appearance.

The recipe

Aunt Ellen starts in a very chatty, informal way, by referring to one of her readers, who sent in a recipe the week before:

> *Two weeks ago, Nancy gave us a recipe for pan haggis (in distinction I presume to the real haggis which was originally cooked in a cow's stomach – or was it the tripe of pig? I have no cookery book to hand) and it reminded me of the haggis I remember my mother making in a pan for a winter breakfast dish. I cannot give the proportions but I remember watching the preparation of it with such interest that I can repeat the process with exactitude.*

> *The suet was cut or grated very fine, and hung high over an open fire to melt slowly – a very little water being added at first to prevent the possibility of burning or hardening. Meanwhile, oatmeal and flour in equal proportions were mixed to a batter with milk, salt and pepper to season being added. When the suet was thoroughly rendered the batter was stirred into it and stirred well so that the whole mass was of a smooth consistency. The pan was again hung very high and the contents left to simmer very gently for an hour or two.*

> *As far as I remember, slices of this, for it hardens when cold, were cut and heated gently for the morning meal.*

This recipe's name is very like the northern panhaggelty, chiefly because they were both cooked in a pan. The similarity ends there, but it is interesting to see how the heat from an open fire could be regulated in quite a sophisticated way, depending on how high the pan was hung above the flames.

Now, on to our familiar panhaggelty. The essence of the dish seems to have been to get a serviceable pan, fling into it the potatoes, other vegetables and bits of meat that were left over from Sunday dinner, and then cook the whole lot in a stock. If there was no meat left over, then sausages could be pressed into service. Panhaggelty could be served on a Monday lunchtime, as it was relatively easy for the housewife to prepare while doing the weekly wash, but Heather Morgan remembers that her family used to go to the Sunday evening service, at their local church, then walk home and tuck into panhaggelty. The dish was delicious and had the advantage of using up every scrap of food left over from Sunday dinner.

My husband remembers his mother cooking the dish and substituting corned beef if there was no left over meat. He says he believes it was possible to eat panhaggelty on a Sunday evening but he never did. His family always had something different for Sunday supper and panhaggelty for Monday lunch.

Fish

Sir James Crichton-Brown

Living in the north east, it is inevitable that fish will play a major part in our diet as we are never very far away from a fishing boat and fresh fish. *The New Home Encyclopaedia* has this sound advice for working people:

> *The old idea that fish make brain because they contain phosphorus is exploded, but fish has considerable dietetic value. Sir James Crichton-Brown is most insistent 'that for working people of all classes – those who work with their hands – fish is an economical source of the energy necessary to enable them to carry on their work, and that for young children and young persons it furnishes the very stuff that is needed to help them grow healthy and strong'.*

The book goes on to quote some further advice from 'this eminent authority':

> *…the finer varieties of fish, such as sole, turbot and brill at …moderate prices …will be by no means extravagant luxuries in even humble homes. But it is in the coarser finds of fish such as plaice, skate, mackerel,*

> *hake, dabs, sprats, haddock and conger eel, that the great*
> *and hitherto much neglected storehouse of food for the*
> *people is to be found.*

Sir James then goes on to explain that:

> *…acting on the unquestioned truth that arose by any*
> *other name would smell as sweet, the names of various*
> *fish are politely camouflaged when offered for sale. The*
> *naturalist knows of no such species as Rock Salmon, which*
> *is usually the Angler-fish or Wold-fish, both ugly looking*
> *creatures and therefore never exposed whole. The so-called*
> *Torbay sole is the Witch; the Scotch sole is apt to conceal*
> *the identity if not the taste of the Megrim, and smoked*
> *Cod fillets are often neither smoked or cod but merely*
> *Ling or Tusk.*

It may be the result of a sheltered childhood but I have never heard of Ling or Tusk. They sound vicious and disturbing, so hats off to anyone who has attempted to cook them. However, after some research I did find that the Venus Tusk fish is a fish with a firm white flaky flesh and a mild and sweet flavour, which is now mainly found in the northern half of Australia! As for the Ling it is a member of the familiar cod family, and can be found widely distributed around British shores. So maybe not so vicious and disturbing as their names suggest.

Crab and dead man's flesh

Everything Within has, as usual, lots to say about, well everything – fish included. The volume fields seventy three recipes for cooking

Crab and dead man's flesh

fish, as well as some sound advice, and a recipe for dressed crab: 'Empty the shell and mix the flesh with vinegar, mustard, salt and pepper, and a little cayenne. Then put the mixture into the large shell again and serve.' So far so good. Then the writer adds, 'Everyone requires at least *one* lesson in dressing a crab. There are portions – the so-called 'Dead man's flesh' that *must* be taken away.'

Fascinating. I have never heard of the expression 'Dead man's flesh' and nor has anyone else I have spoken to about the subject. And why the italics? What would happen if someone didn't have that one lesson? I think we should be told.

I investigated further and discovered that once a crab dies its flesh deteriorates rapidly and can become toxic. The non-edible flesh being the mouthpiece and the feathery grey gills, the 'dead man's fingers'. However, in spite of the glamorous and terrifying name, they are not actually poisonous, merely tough and indigestible.

'Mock' this and that

As well as recipes for all sorts of crab dishes, people seemed to have had a bit of a mania for making food out of something else and then calling it by another name entirely. For example, *Warne's Model Cookery and Housekeeping Book* has the following recipe:

Mock crab – sailor fashion

The recipe

A large slice of Gloucester cheese
1 teaspoon of mustard
1 teaspoon of vinegar
Pepper and salt to taste

Cut a slice of Gloucester cheese rather thin; but of good
size round. Mash it up with a fork to a paste, mix it with
vinegar, mustard and pepper. It has a great flavour of
crab.

Haddock olives

Warne's Model Cookery and Housekeeping Book has a further recipe
for 'Haddock Olives'.

The recipe

½ lb cooked haddock
2 tablespoons cream
2 hard boiled eggs
1 dessertspoon chopped parsley
A little pepper and cayenne
2 oz breadcrumbs
1 egg
3 oz butter

Pound and chop haddock very fine, work in the cream, hard-boiled eggs, 1 oz butter, pepper and cayenne. Rub through a fine wire sieve. Form into oval shapes the size of olives, brush over with egg, roll in breadcrumbs and fry in butter.

Mock mayonnaise

The recipe for Halibut is followed by one for Mock mayonnaise. The recipe book confides, that when the two are combined they 'make an attractive looking supper dish'.

The recipe

Boil about 3 lb fish. Remove any ugly skin etc. and allow to get quite cold. Make a pint of white sauce; add, when boiled, the whisked yolk of an egg and 1 tablespoon of vinegar. Pour over fish. When cold, decorate prettily with capers.

Mock capers

Other recipes suggest that a handy substitute for capers could be nasturtium seeds. Indeed, nasturtium leaves and flowers can be used in salads, sauces and sandwiches. The leaves are as hot as mustard and the flowers sweet yet peppery and if the seeds are pickled, they can pass as capers!

We could go on forever, substituting this ingredient for that until the dish made no sense whatsoever. Here is one last 'mock' from the

Thompson scrap-book – which appears in 'Alice in Wonderland',
not as a recipe, but a character, the Mock Turtle.

Mock turtle soup

The recipe

To a cleaned, uncooked ox foot add two quarts of water
in which beef has been boiled. Simmer gently until the
foot is tender, then slip the flesh off the bones and
replace the bones in the stock. Continue the slow boiling
for another hour, then strain, put aside until cold and
remove the fat. Two hours beforehand reheat the stock
with more stock or water to increase the measure to three
pints. When boiling add a level tablespoonful of very
small dice of onion and a larger one of diced carrot, and
just a little celery in small dice. When the vegetables have
boiled for ten minutes add the ox foot in rather large dice
and before the vegetables are soft enough to break,
thicken the soup with moistened arrowroot. Season to
taste and add a little sherry before serving.

Fish and potato pie

The plentiful nature of fish in the north east, meant that whole
families could earn a living from the sea. An old lady from
Cullercoats, living at St Anne's Residential Home, said that her dad
would go out and catch crabs and fish then bring them home to
his wife who made them into fish and crab cakes, and fish pies.
'She would go out, dressed in her black dress, hat and shawl, carrying

her pies and cakes in a basket. She took the train to Ovington and sold the pies and fish cakes then would walk up Prudhoe Bank to sell in the town. After that she would walk along to Crawcrook and Blaydon where she would get the train to Cullercoats. The money she made would go towards the housekeeping but she would often buy a gift for me from a little shop in Blaydon. I remember getting a brooch which had flowers and birds on it.'

The recipe

>   1 lb boiled potatoes
>   1 oz butter
>   Teaspoon chopped parsley
>   Salt and pepper
>   ½ boiled fish
>   ½ pint fish stock

>   Remove skin and bone from fish and flake it. Grease pie dish and put fish in dish with stock. Sprinkle with pepper. Mash the potatoes with butter, pepper and salt, add the chopped parsley. Cover fish with potatoes and bake for 20 minutes in a moderate oven, or until nicely browned.

Catholics, fish and the war

Ann Edgar remembers coming home from school to the delicious smell of freshly baked bread and cakes on baking day. After the oven had cooled down, her mother would cook a great bowl of herrings which she had first gutted, stuffed with onions, then rolled up and covered with vinegar, cloves and spices. This dish was cooked until it had a golden, crispy topping which Mrs Edgar says was 'very attractive'.

Mrs Edgar recalls that Catholics all ate fish on a Friday as a matter of religious observance. However, during the Second World War the Pope issued a dispensation which allowed Catholics to eat meat on a Friday if they couldn't get fish. Fishing boats and crews were busy fighting Hitler, and the Pope obviously felt that he had to do his bit to encourage people in England not to be too rigid about the Fish on Friday edict.

Mrs Edgar says that families usually just had one wage coming in. She was the wife of a policemen and the police force would not allow a wife to work, while women who worked in offices and as teachers had to give up their jobs when they got married. Businesses would not employ married women, but would sometimes employ widows. The war, explained Mrs Edgar, changed all of that.

And two veg

Today we like to think that we've got it about right. We are recommended to eat five portions of fruit and vegetables per day in order to stay healthy. We're not quite sure why that is such a good idea but we are prepared to follow it when it suits us. However, we could do no better than consult the Thompson scrap-book for a further explanation on the efficacy of vegetables.

Vegetables and worn nerves

> Eat lettuce and onions for worn nerves. Beets and turnips give iron to the blood. Tomatoes stimulate a torpid liver. Celery is good for rheumatism. Beetroots are nourishing and laxative. Carrots cleanse the blood and clear the complexion. Asparagus is beneficial to the kidneys. All kinds of greens in spring help to cleanse the blood and regulate the system.

Well, that's pretty thorough. The bit I like best is lettuce and onions for worn nerves. I don't know how it works, or even what constitutes a 'worn nerve', but it sounds just the job.

Peas in turnip cases

What with television cooks, cookery magazines and cookery books we think ourselves pretty cosmopolitan these days and rarely baulk at unusual and some would say downright perverse combinations of food. However, when I came across the following recipe from the Thompson family scrap-book I was alarmed by the sheer volume of butter needed and the strange concept of serving peas and turnips in one small dish.

The recipe

Peel six medium sized white turnips and remove the centres with a strong spoon or a vegetable cutter leaving a shell about ¼ inch thick. Cook in boiling salted water for about twenty five minutes or until tender. Drain thoroughly and put on a hot plate. Mix two cupfuls of peas with four tablespoons of butter, one half teaspoon of salt and one eighth teaspoon of pepper. Heat in a double boiler and use to fill the turnip cups. The peas may be mixed with one cupful of well seasoned white sauce if desired or the sauce may be poured round the turnip. If a vegetable cutter is used, boil the turnip balls, roll in chopped parsley and use as a garnish.

Brussels sprout soup – yes really!

And now for something completely appalling! Is there a vegetable that you would never, under any circumstances eat because it tastes like dirty dishwater? For me it has to be the humble brussels sprout.

Now, can you think of anything which would make the sprout taste even worse than it does normally? No? Well read on.

Brussels sprout soup, courtesy of *Modern Cookery Illustrated*:

The recipe

2 lb Brussels sprouts
2 pints white stock, or meat broth
Pinch of bicarbonate of soda
½ pint milk
1 dessertspoon cornflour
Salt and pepper
Grating of nutmeg

Trim and wash sprouts, put in a pan of boiling water with small teaspoonful of salt and bicarbonate of soda. Bring to the boil, and boil for five minutes. Remove the scum. Then strain in a colander.

Put stock in a stewpot. When it boils add the sprouts and boil until they are quite soft – about ten minutes – then rub them through a sieve. Return the puree and stock to the stewpan. Mix the cornflour to a very thin paste with milk. Stir it into the soup and continue stirring until it has boiled for five minutes. Season to taste with salt and pepper. Add nutmeg and remainder of milk. Make very hot and serve.

Just in case anyone has doubts about serving such an obnoxious dish, *Modern Cookery Illustrated* adds, 'this soup is particularly good for children who dislike green vegetables, as it enables them to assimilate the valuable mineral salts in a more palatable form.'

Well, I don't know about you, but boiling sprouts, adding them to stock, then sieving them and thickening with cornflour and water does not make the idea any more appetising. That, however, is my personal feeling about Brussels sprouts and in their defence they are very nutritious and rich in vitamin C.

If you don't share my views on sprouts, and think they are the bees knees, there is a British Sprout Growers Association (www.sprouts.uk.com) to keep you up to date with all sprout related matters.

Pease pudding

Pease pudding has always been a much loved northern dish, as it can be served with ham, in sandwiches, with sausages, hot or cold, and is a great comfort to toddlers who have been out shopping for too long and can only be comforted with a saveloy dip laced generously with pease pudding. The dish is easy to make and relatively fool proof, as long as you remember to rinse the spilt peas after steeping them in bicarbonate of soda and not just cook them in the same water, as my husband and I did on one occasion when we were entertaining his family for the first time after we were married.

The recipe

½ lb spilt peas
Salt and pepper
1 oz butter or margarine (optional)
1 egg (optional)

Wash peas thoroughly and discard black ones. Soak them
in cold water overnight. Then put them in a cloth and
tie rather loosely so that they have plenty of room to
swell. Plunge them into boiling water that has had ½
teaspoonful of salt added to it. Then boil until they are
tender – about two and a half hours. Take them out of
the cloth and rub them through a coarse sieve. Season
with salt and pepper then tie tightly in a cloth and boil
for another half hour. If the pudding is to be served with
boiled pork or any boiled meat, it should be put in with
the meat for the second boiling, as the broth will very
much improve the flavour. If, however, the pudding is to
be served alone, add the butter or margarine and a well
beaten egg, after rubbing the peas through the sieve.

Originally the dish would be made with whole peas which were
put in a sack with a sprig of mint then left to simmer in the pot
along with a cut of meat.

In the nineteenth century, 'Pease Pudding Hot…' was sold by
street vendors in and around Newcastle.

Leek pudding

Leek pudding similarly causes people's eyes to glaze over with contentment, and remember a time when people didn't have much money and had to make filling and nutritious food on very little money. Leek pudding was made from suet pastry, which was rolled out, fitted into a pudding basin, and then filled with leeks, chopped up small. A suet lid was then placed over the pudding which was steamed for a couple of hours. The pudding could also be made in a cloth, but if this was the case then the leeks were mixed with the suet pastry mix, the whole lot was wrapped in cloth and suspended in boiling water for the requisite amount of time.

Leeks are still very popular and are grown for food, and competitively, throughout the region.

Baked onions with mustard

I had never heard of the delicacy which is baked onions with mustard, but several friends remember their fathers enjoying a baked onion, accompanied either by cheese or mustard. The mustard combination had the added benefit according to Ruth Hearn's father, of being instrumental in enabling you to sweat out a cold.

Lilian Bianchi says that her father liked Spanish onions, chopped, boiled and served with butter, salt and pepper, as a dish for supper. 'He was perfectly happy so long as he had three good meals and a bite of supper.'

Like the Brussels sprout, onions are rather understated. Modern medical research indicates that onions may help guard against many chronic diseases such as cataracts, cardiovascular disease and cancer.

Beetroot and white sauce

Beetroot and white sauce was unknown to me, but was apparently a delicacy and could be served as a vegetable to accompany meat or fish.

Beetroot is in fact enjoying a revival in some fashionable restaurants and its health-giving properties are being recognised too. As it is rich in vitamins and minerals, particularly iron and magnesium, it can be used to treat anaemia and conditions involving the blood and immune system.

Potatoes and Vienna

Potatoes do not conjure up a picture of sophistication and continental cuisine, but the *Sunday Pictorial* of 1 November 1942 suggests that the British have much to learn, vis-à-vis the potato, from the Viennese. The advert for potatoes begins, 'In Vienna then…In England now' and goes on to explain:

> *When Vienna was still a city of song, the excellence of its food was known throughout the world. In those carefree days, Wiener schnitzel – veal slices dipped in egg and crumb, fried in butter, was a popular Viennese dish. Potato cookery too was carried to a fine art in Vienna. The other day a team of Viennese cooks made a special*

Potatoes and Vienna

potato breakfast dish in London. Try it yourself. It is a
simple recipe and it makes good use of our home grown
potatoes – the splendid crop that saves our ships.

Wartime Britain was being encouraged to make do and mend, to
be content with what crops could be grown at home and not yearn
for foreign food which had to be imported. There follows a recipe
for Viennese fish cakes, with, no surprises here, not a hint of fish
but plenty of potatoes!

Viennese fish cakes

The recipe

Cooking time, 15 mins
½ lb of boiled, mashed potatoes
½ teaspoon dried egg
½ teaspoon anchovy essence
1 tablespoon breadcrumbs
Pepper and salt to taste

Mix all the ingredients together and form into little
cakes. Fry in a little fat until golden brown on both sides.

The advert finishes off with the stirring words, 'Potatoes are part of
the battle', stirring sentiments, and furthermore, entirely true.
During war time it was no good hankering for what you couldn't
have, you had to get used to cooking with basic ingredients.

Puddings

Oh no, I really shouldn't – oh well alright then.

We have a complex relationship with puddings today and I challenge anyone to pick up a single magazine from a news-stand which does not include an article about:

(a) diets;

(b) obesity;

(c) diets and obesity.

Magazine writers and editors, if all of the articles can be believed, are anxious about the nations' weight, and concerned that we:

(a) don't get too fat;

(b) don't get too thin;

(c) don't get both too fat and too thin.

It is difficult to know how to reconcile these opposing views but the fact remains, magazines jump off the shelves when they report a new diet.

Years ago, people didn't concern themselves overly with being fat, thin or just right. Fuel intake and energy output just about matched and people had other things to worry about. Weight tended to be treated with a degree of insouciance which we would find alarming today.

I was interested therefore to find a couple of sentences about 'thin children' in the Thompson scrap-book. The paragraph was at the end of a series of short hints and tips, following advice about how to salt fish, whiten clothes, treat a burn with powdered charcoal, clean mother of pearl, take creases out of velvet, and, by using sliced raw onions in a sick room, prevent disease from being spread:

> *Thin children – a child may be well nourished and in perfect health without being fat. If the body is supplied with more food than it needs and can utilise at the moment, the excess is stored, usually in the shape of fat. There may be no surplus and yet the necessary wants of the body may be fully met. Firm well-developed muscle is better than fat.*

And there we have it, in a nutshell. No need to read slimming magazines or pay good money to attend a slimming class, simply do not over eat!

Milk puddings – semolina, ground rice, tapioca, sago, and macaroni puddings

Barley was used for a sweet pudding, well soaked in water. Milk, sugar and raisins were added, and then the pudding was baked in the oven for a couple of hours.

Macaroni was also used for puddings rather than as a savoury dish. The Co-Op sold a brand called 'Finest Horseshoe Brand Macaroni', and the long sticks were broken into two or three pieces. An uncle of mine, as a child, liked to get a tube of macaroni which was baked hard, off the top of the pudding, and suck the milk up as if through a straw. Happy days.

Lilian Bianchi says that her grandmother, Granny Carr, used to put an egg into the rice pudding as she was baking it. This addition may have made the rice pudding more nutritious and filling, but it was very firm and not very nice to eat.

The Co-Op also sold 'Pure Semolina Wheat Preparation Guaranteed Pure' which was displayed as 'A popular and nutritious Article of Diet.'

The recipe

2 oz semolina or ground rice, tapioca, sago, macaroni
1 pint milk
1 oz sugar
1 strip of lemon peel
Grated nutmeg
½ oz butter

Put the chosen grains into a buttered two pint ovenproof
dish and stir in the milk. Add the sugar and lemon rind
and stir. Sprinkle with grated nutmeg and dot with butter.

Bake in the oven at 150c 300f gas 2 for 2-2 ½ hrs. Stir it
after 30 minutes.

Sago cream

We tend not to eat much sago today. However, here is a recipe from
The Thompson scrap-book which sounds quite palatable and
appears to have been cooked over an open fire, probably on a large
black range.

The recipe

½ pint milk
Yolk of one egg
1 oz fine sago
½ oz of fine sugar
Pinch of salt

Wash the sago several times, then soak about fifteen
minutes in a little milk. Put the remainder of the milk
into a white-lined pan, allow it to get hot, then add the
sago and salt, and cook over the fire until it is
transparent, stirring all the time. Allow it to cool a little,
then mix the yolk and sugar together in a basin, pour
into the sago stirring continuously; then it is ready for
use. This is very nice to eat cold. It may be poured into a
wet mould, stand until cold, turned out and served with
stewed fruit or jam.

Baked custard

The recipe

1 pint milk
3 eggs
2 level tablespoons sugar
Grated nutmeg

Warm the milk in a saucepan but do not boil. Whisk the eggs and sugar lightly in a bowl.

Pour on the hot milk stirring all the time.

Strain the mixture into a buttered ovenproof dish.

Sprinkle the nutmeg on the top and bake in the oven at 170c, 325f, gas 3 for 45 minutes or until firm to the touch.

Serve cold.

Yorkshire puddings

There was an often repeated saying in the north which goes something like this, 'Them that eats the most pudding gets the most meat.'

Yorkshire puddings were often served before the meat and vegetables, accompanied by gravy or sometimes jam and I am led to believe that in Lincolnshire, puddings were served with raspberry vinegar. The idea behind serving the puddings first was that people would fill up on the least expensive food, and not crave too much of that expensive commodity, roast beef.

The recipe

5 oz flour
1 pint milk
Pinch of salt
2 eggs
2 tablespoons of hot dripping

Mix salt with flour and put through a fine sieve. (This is very important, according to *Modern Cookery Illustrated*, because it helps to create a perfectly smooth batter.) Separate the whites from the yolks, make a well in the centre of the flour and drop in the whole yolks. Mix a little of the flour then very gradually add half a pint of milk, mixing the remainder of the dry flour until the mixture is perfectly smooth. Beat well for about eight minutes and then add the rest of the milk. Leave for an hour then add the beaten egg whites just before baking. When the mixture is ready pour into the hot dripping in the Yorkshire pudding tin and bake in a hot oven for 30-40 minutes.

I know of no-one who has ever beaten a Yorkshire pudding mixture for eight minutes. We would probably have a heart attack at the thought today. It is interesting to note that the author of *Modern Cookery Illustrated* acknowledges 'with thanks', the help of the Medical Research Council. I expect they were interested in the after effects of all that beating.

Coconut haystacks

The recipe

8 oz desiccated coconut
2 oz caster sugar
1 egg
4 glazed cherries

Mix coconut and sugar together in a mixing bowl.
Beat the egg thoroughly and add to the mixture.
Form the mixture into individual haystack shapes using
an egg cup (lightly press some of the mixture into an egg
cup and tap the shape out onto a lightly greased baking
tray).
Repeat this procedure until all the mixture has been
used.

Top each haystack with half a cherry.

Bake in the centre of the oven 150c, 300f, gas 2 for 10-
15 minutes or until golden brown.

Lemon jelly

This is a recipe I found in *Enquire within upon Everything*. The
recipe appears quite complicated and intrigued me because it
involves something called 'isinglass' which I subsequently discovered
is a form of gelatine. Complicated or not, the book recommends it
unhesitatingly.

The recipe

For a quart mould – dissolve two ounces of isinglass in
1¾ pints of water; strain it and add ¾ lb sifted loaf sugar,
the juice of 6 lemons and the rind of one; boil for a few
minuets and strain it again then let it stand until it is
quite cold and beginning to stiffen; then beat the whites
of two eggs and add, whisk till it is white; put in a mould
which must first be wetted with cold water – or salad oil
is a much better substitute for turning out jelly.
However, great care must be taken not to pour the lemon
mixture into the mould until it is quite cool or the oil will
float to the top. After it is turned out it must be carefully
wiped over with a clean cloth.

According to the recipe book, 'This plan only needs to be tried
once to be invariably adopted.' What confidence in the product.

Apple tart

Once again, from the same book of household hints, comes this
particularly odd sounding recipe for pastry.

The recipe

1 lb flour
2 drachms[4] bicarbonate of soda
2 drachms muriatic acid

---

[4] 8 drachms = 1 ounce/480 grains. 8fl. ounce drachms = 1fl. Ounce.

6 oz butter
Water – enough to bring it to the consistence required.

This terse little recipe is followed by detailed instructions regarding the preparation of the apples.

> Peel, core and quarter the apples; boil the cores and parings in sugar and water; strain off the liquor, adding more sugar; grate the rind of a lemon over the apples and squeeze the juice into the syrup; mix 6 cloves with the fruit, put in a piece of butter the size of a walnut; cover with pastry.

Banana refuse

While this is not strictly a recipe, in fact it is not in any way a recipe, I found it in the Thompson scrap-book and couldn't resist putting it into this book. The full heading for the tip was 'Banana refuse makes paper' and I couldn't for the life of me imagine what two sisters living in a farm in Northumberland could do with this tip. They must have thought it sufficiently useful to cut out, store and then paste into their household hints book. I can't, equally, think what readers of this book could do with the hint, but included it all the same in the interests of strangeness.

> *Good paper can be made from banana refuse. The trash or refuse consisting of the stems of banana trees, from which the fruit has been cut, is run through crushing rolls, which produces a mash, in which the moisture has been reduced from 90-55-75%. The pulping machine reduces the mixture to pulp and the pulp and juice are*

boiled and beaten. The removal of the fibrous material from the beater completes the process in which no chemical is used.

Spotted dick

The recipe

1 lb self raising flour
1 teaspoon baking powder
½ lb lard or margarine or dripping
Pinch of salt
1 oz granulated sugar
4 oz currants or seedless raisins

Mix salt, baking powder and flour together. Rub in the fat until evenly distributed and mix with very cold water to make soft dough. Roll out, sprinkle the currants and sugar over it. Roll up as you would a roly-poly. Tie in a cloth and boil for three hours.

Bread boily

Pat Stoneman of Blyth has an interesting 'poor man's fast food' recipe, 'Bread boily'. Mrs Stoneman says that this dish used to be served up to children on cold winter nights and was made from chunks of stale bread, scalded with boiling milk, with sugar added to sweeten, put in an enamel dish and placed in front of a coal fire, on a little cracket. The 'Bread boily' slowly heated up and, according to Mrs Stoneman, 'made you sleep like a top, and was cheaper than the snack foods which are so popular now'. Pat points out that the dish had excellent nutritional values: 'Calcium, protein, fibre, carbohydrate. And it tasted lovely with my mam's home-made bread and the full cream milk from those days.'

Treacle tart

This is a recipe from an old *Bero* book, which was the bible of cookery at one time.

The recipe

8 oz plain flour
4 oz butter or margarine
Pinch of salt
2 tablespoons very cold water
4 oz golden syrup
1 oz breadcrumbs
1 oz butter

Mix salt and flour into a large bowl.
Cut the fat into small pieces and then lightly rub into the flour until the mixture resembles breadcrumbs.

Add the cold water very gradually until a soft dough forms. Roll out the pastry onto a floured surface and line a tin in the same way as for jam tarts.

Sprinkle half the breadcrumbs onto the pastry then add a layer of syrup, and top with the remaining breadcrumbs. Dot with small pieces of butter.

Bake at 200c, 400f, gas 6 until the pastry is golden
brown. Serve either hot or cold.

Empire Christmas Pudding

Mrs Underwood of Howdon, Wallsend, has a wonderful recipe for
'Empire Christmas Pudding' which was used by her mother, 'Every
year she would make the mixture, having collected the fruit over a
period of weeks. Her brothers and sisters all received one of her
puddings as part of their Christmas present, usually with a knitted
teapot cosy or home made apron.'

The recipe is one which has been cut out of the *Daily Mail*
newspaper from 21 November 1929, and proudly states, 'This
Daily Mail recipe which has been invented and thoroughly tested
by the Lord Mayor's chef, will make a valuable addition to your
cookery book. Cut it out and keep it for reference.' The recipe has
lasted for seventy years, and I bet it still works as well as when Mrs
Underwood's mother was making puddings for her family, all those
years ago.

The recipe

1 lb beef suet Scotland
½ lb flour Australia
1 lb breadcrumbs England
1 lb currants Australia
1 lb sultanas Australia
1 lb raisins South Africa
½ lb lexias (muscatels) Australia
½ lb mixed peel South Africa

1 nutmeg Straits Settlements
½ teaspoon mixed spice Malaya
Juice of one lemon Dominica
8 eggs New Zealand
½ lb sugar Jamaica
A little salt England
½ gill brandy Cyprus
¼ gill rum Jamaica

The newspaper article continues, 'Last year the Lord Mayor of London's chef made 57 lb of Christmas Pudding with all Empire ingredients, using the King's recipe. This year he has given to *The Daily Mail* his own special Empire recipe, which is suitable for a private household.'

The chef goes on to give a few tips to the domestic cook:

A Chef's Tips

Mix all the ingredients one week before cooking.

Mix suet, flour and dried fruit together, then sugar, breadcrumbs, spice, lemon and orange juice, and third, the eggs, rum and brandy. Finally, mix all together.

If the mixture seems too thick then add a little milk.

Boil very slowly. Many cooks imagine, erroneously, that temperature rises with quick boiling.

Always give Christmas puddings six to eight hours slow boiling. If the puddings are steamed in the steamer, allow two hours longer.

Brandy sauce is the best in this connection. Mix with a whip, ¼ lb of soft, not melted, butter and a little caster sugar, adding, at the same time and very slowly, a wineglassful of South African or Cyprus brandy.

This recipe is interesting because the quantities are vast, and the article displays a jaunty optimism about the ingredients and the pudding. The pudding was created by the Lord Mayor of London's chef, so it must be good. The ingredients are all from the British Empire, so they must be good, and the recipe assumes that the cooks are solid British citizens, with eight or ten hours of spare time, ready to devote to the making of a Christmas pudding fit for a King. Today, we panic a bit if something can't be microwaved in ten minutes. Imagine devoting ten hours to one dish. It seems odd now, but people cooked partly because they had to, and partly because it was an enjoyable and rewarding occupation. And there's still nothing to beat receiving a home-made present at Christmas.

Empire Christmas Pudding

Bought food

Our grandmothers and mothers used to have incredibly busy and strenuous lives, cooking all manner of nourishing and hearty foods, and still found time to make cakes, pastries and biscuits on the side.

I can remember my mother being appalled by the thought of buying cakes and biscuits, the only exception being a trip down Fort Street in South Shields, to a bread shop called 'Kerr's' who sold all sorts of fancy cakes like macaroons, marzipan cauliflowers, jap cakes and cream horns. These cakes were special and were bought only for Sunday tea, to help us ward off the pangs of hunger between our substantial Sunday dinner and our glorious fry-up after church.

However, if biscuits were bought, then it was odds on that they had been made at Wright's Biscuit Factory, home of 'Family Creams', 'Osborne', 'Iced Fluted' and 'Thin Wine'.

If you remember all of these biscuits, you really did have a sweet tooth, or you, or someone in your family, probably worked at Wright's Biscuit factory in 1959.

If you remember delicious sounding treats like 'Miranda', 'Army Bread' or 'Iron Rations', then you probably worked at the factory during the Second World War.

If you remember the following biscuits, 'Durham Creams', 'Snips' (North Eastern) or 'Maple Crunch', then you probably worked at Wright's in 1939, immediately prior to the war.

Wright's Biscuits

A lovely old lady called Mrs McNamee of South Shields, who sadly is no longer alive, had lots of stories to tell about working at Wright's Biscuit Factory and the many happy memories of her time there. She was one of the first ten people to start work at Wright's Biscuit Factory in June 1933, when it was opened by Mr Webster and Mr Cross who came especially from Lancashire to start the task of keeping Shields people and other folks in the north east, supplied with biscuits.

I wrote an article for the *Shields Gazette* about working at Wright's, and since then people have accosted me in the most unlikely places, wanting to share their memories of the factory and the companionship which existed there. Many women worked there for years, but it was not unusual for a woman to work for a fortnight, to pay off an outstanding bill.

My mother-in-law, Louisa Cooke, worked at the factory with her sister, Vera. She said that she was worried when she first got the job, because, 'Some of the women are supposed to be very rough. They have fights.' However, when she got to the factory, put on her overall and hairnet and got started on the Jammy Dodgers, Custard

Creams and Marshmallows, she found the work hard and hot, but the company was sweet.

Mrs McNamee's husband started at the factory in 1934, and very soon they were walking out together, one of thirteen couples who met in the bakehouse, and married. Mrs McNamee treasures a book of hand-written biscuit and cake recipes, which belonged to her husband, who worked as the production manager. The book was handed down to him from a former production manager, and was already half full of recipes. Mr McNamee added recipes as he progressed, and the book also provides us with some details about recipe trials. Unfortunately, recipes dating from 1933-1939 have been removed from the record so we'll never know their names or ingredients…unless someone can remember.

Here are some lists of ingredients, and if you worked at Wright's Biscuit Factory any time between 1939 and the closure in 1972, there's a good chance that you worked on some of these assorted fancies. The quantities are huge and some of the ingredients are strange… but interesting.

Golden Crunch 1939

The ingredients

> 29 lb of sugar – fine granulated
> 1 lb of raisins – Californian Naturals
> 13 lb fat – 8 of Promex
> 15 lb oats – small flake breakfast
> 22 lb flour – 8 lb of Australian pastry flour

24 drams – vanilla essence (1:5 water)
13 drams – butter flavour – undiluted
12 drams cinnamon
26 drams gun
4½ pints water (added to oats)
1 pint water (added to gun)

The ingredients seem pretty incomprehensible to me, looking down over the years. What, for example is 'gun'. It sounds pretty lethal, and I make a mental note to steer clear of any biscuits I see called 'Golden Crunch'. However, Mrs McNamee had the soothing answer: 'gun' appears to have been a finely sifted mix of 1¾ lb of brown sugar, 5 lb of soda and 5¼ lb of salt. The list ends with the note that the 'vanilla flavour (American type) is supplied by Messrs. Stevenson and Howell Ltd. of London', and the 'butter flavour (butter flavour?) is supplied by Messrs Langdale, London' and was 'a pineapple essence in a maize oil base, specially prepared'.

You might like to decipher the following list of ingredients:

Snips (North Eastern)

The ingredients

280 lb Canadian
140 lb Winter
140 lb Hogarth
1 lb Comp or W.O.
5 lb brown sugar
5 lb puratose

14 lb salt
7 lb yeast

Mrs MacNamee explained. 'Canadian', 'Winter' and 'Hogarth' are all types of flour. 'Comp' or 'W.O.' is a mystery, but 'puratose' was a pink colouring, which was used in this recipe as well as in the recipe for pink marshmallow biscuits.

Army bread

Army bread was made during the war.

The ingredients

280 lb wheatmeal
140 lb flour
28 lb brown sugar
15 lb milk powder
2 lb 4 oz salt
3 lb soda
1½ lb vol
13-14 gallons warm water

'Vol' was a raising agent, like bicarbonate of soda.

The note at the end of this recipe adds:

> *Makes 12-16 packets with 48 packets to a tin. There should be 4% moisture in the biscuit after baking.*

This suggests that the Army bread was some sort of army biscuit, which could be stored and used as needed. Apparently the biscuits were made throughout the war and were horrible: hard, like roofing tiles, and not tasting of much either.

Burned biscuits

For as long as anyone can remember, the people who worked at Wright's were proud of the chimney, it was a landmark and a reminder of hard work and good times. When staff at the factory came back from their holidays, if they could afford holidays, the first thing they saw was the factory chimney, and the first thing they smelled, if they lived nearby, was the smell of gingersnaps, comforting, warm, sometimes burned. Jim Lawson remembers living in Vine Street, near the factory. His mother, Belle Lawson, would go outside to put the washing out to dry and smell burned biscuits. She would tell Jim, 'Get up the street and stand in the queue for the burned biscuits. I'll bring some coppers along soon. There'll be loads going today.' Jim was reluctant to queue as some of the women shouted out comments designed to embarrass a young boy, and he was always scared that he'd get to the front of the queue before his mother arrived with the money to pay for his order.

Marshmallow biscuits

These biscuits were very popular. One girl, working on her own, made them at the top of the building, three storeys up.

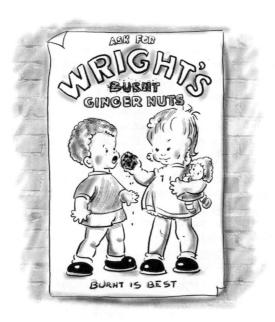

Burned Biscuits

The recipe

Topping for Marshmallow:

> 130 lb sugar
> 70 lb glucose
> 90 lb invert sugar
> 4½ gallons water

> Put the sugar and water in a kettle and heat to nearly boiling point. Add invert sugar, stirring until all of the mixture is dissolved. Turn off heat and add glucose, stirring in well. Finally flush the whole mass through a fine copper sieve, into suitable storage tanks. Then take 34 lbs of the above syrup, add to it 12½ oz of gelatine which has been dissolved in 1½-2 pints of water. Whisk for about 12 minutes. Add colouring and flavouring last.

> It should not be overbeaten, as this will cause the marshmallow to break down and toughen up.

'Invert sugar' was the name given to sugar, which had been heated and turned into liquid.

Marshmallow biscuits were obviously a great favourite with the public, as Wright's appear to have been constantly adapting the recipe. Mrs MacNamee's book contains six recipes for the marshmallow topping, the first one recorded in July 1939 and the last in September 1950, all with very little variation but all striving towards that perfect marshmallow biscuit. Perhaps they got there in the end.

Here's another marshmallow recipe. It is the first one recorded and is perhaps the most sophisticated as it takes weather conditions into account.

Marshmallow (Lavery's)

The recipe

85 gall water
125 lb Tate's seconds sugar
32 lb invert sugar
26 lb glucose
4 oz vanilla essence

Dissolve gelatine in ten quarts of the water. Put other ingredients in steam pan and heat to 100 Fahrenheit. Add gelatine and water and take to 175 F. Pour into containers and when set, remove skin carefully in one piece. The resulting jelly should be broken down in a strong machine with the beater before being whisked.

IMPORTANT

1. Use finest quality gelatine (powder).

2. Sugar should be hard.

3. Adhere to temperatures.

4. No grease in pan or beater.

[The recipe continues]

3 lb puratose
3 lb sugar
4 lb glucose
½ cream of tartar
26 oz water

Boil up, and if weather is warm, add 8 ozs gelatine and
2½ pints of boiling water. If weather is cold, reduce
gelatine by ½ oz.

[The recipe further adds]

Jam for above:

8 oz Aga Aga
6 pints cold water
6 lb sugar
4 pints cold water
6 lb jam
8 oz cornflour

Boil Aga Aga and then boil sugar. When sugar is boiled
add Aga Aga and boil together. Mix jam and cornflour to
a paste, add to above and boil. Add essence and
colouring.

What then, is Aga Aga? Even Mrs MacNamee admitted that she
was beat.

Almond macaroon

Another favourite was the Almond macaroon. A letter has been preserved from The European Export Company Ltd. to W. P. Webster Esq. of Messrs, Wright's Biscuits Ltd. The letter is dated 21 October 1953 and reads:

> *Our Principals state that by following this recipe and baking the goods in a band oven, a first class Almond Macaroon will result, and we would be very grateful to hear whether upon this information you may now be prepared to commence your experiments for the introduction to the market of an Almond Macaroon Biscuit.*

The biscuit really deserves a fanfare, after such a rousing call to action.

Flying saucers

The ingredients

560 lb biscuit flour
131 lb caster sugar
50 lb granulated sugar
140 lb compound or biscuit fat
28 lb margarine
10 lb syrup
30 lb glucose
6 lb salt
4 lb soda

1 lb tartric acid
4 oz butter essence
4 oz vanilla essence
5-5¼ gallon water

Flying saucers were remembered by my mother-in-law, with much agony. They were well named, and when they came out of the oven, they were so hot and round that they were a devil to catch and pack!